Little Bear and the Mirror

This is the season for the children! Your story sings to the heart,
the song of light we know but can scarcely believe - yet.
Dr. C Baxter Kruger, Author & Teacher

Little Bear and The Mirror
is dedicated to our amazing
grandchildren Nicola and Christiaan
and to all the children of the world!

Little Bear
and
The Mirror

Lydia du Toit and her husband Francois married in January 1979 and live in South Africa. They have four children and two grandchildren.

"I think my imagination for story telling started in my early childhood. We lived like gypsies in a caravan and traveled criss cross our beautiful country wherever my Pappa's work would take him. Long before any TV, and often so remote, that even the radio didn't work, we invented stories and created places, yet to be discovered, at night around the campfires, or in bed, entertained with my Mamma's amazing stories, taking us with her to Neverland. CS Lewis, as well as Elizabeth Goudge were some of my favorite authors. Raising our 4 children, I remember Francois often listening in and urging me to write these unfolding stories down one day! There is wonderful, hidden world, waiting to be explored in every child's mind. I trust that *Little Bear and The Mirror* will unlock a most beautiful, safe place for all who read it."
www.mirrorword.net

Karlee Lillywhite is an illustrator who lives in Ithaca, NY with her husband and cat. She is passionate about visual storytelling that inspires wonder.
Hiraethillustrations.com

Godfrey Birtill is a very gifted musician/composer who travels the world with his wonderful music. He originates from Lancashire, is now living in Eagle, Lincolnshire and has been married for 33 years to Gill. They have four children and seven grandchildren.
Godfrey composed the melody and beautifully sings the Mirror Song that Lydia wrote.
www.godfreyb.com

The Little Bear and the Mirror is also translated by *Davina Langner* into German and *Lilia Kane* into Spanish.
Thank you to *Bess Rhoades* for your encouragements and help with the editing.
Also, *Jacqueline du Toit* and *Sean Osmond* with final layout and preparations for print and Kindle.

Published by Mirror Word Publishing and Lightning Source

Behold how beautiful,
how valuable and
how loved you are.

Anyone who hears this word
sees the face of their true likeness, as in a mirror!

James 1:23 Mirror Bible.

For a free audio download of the book, as well as the Mirror song,
visit: www.mirrorword.net

Little Bear and the Mirror

"Why are you so cold and shivering?" Squirrel asked Little Bear, who was lying curled up in a bundle under the big elm tree.

"Oh, I am so cold and shivering because I am scared," answered Little Bear, with a tremor in his voice.

"My goodness!" said Squirrel, "Why are you scared?"

"Oh, I fear the strange noise I can hear in the forest trees. It makes my hair stand on end and my teeth chatter with cold. I think I need a blanket that will help me get nice and warm," said Little Bear with big, wide eyes.

"Let me see what I can do," said friendly Squirrel and scurried into the forest to find a blanket for Little Bear. Soon, he found some friends who helped him make a blanket for Little Bear.

Porcupine obliged and gave them two of his long sharp quills. Big Oak gave some leaves and bark for the new blanket. They worked together to make holes in the bark with the quills and then stuck the leaves in neat rows up and down the bark. It didn't look very warm and comfortable, but Squirrel excitedly took the leafy blanket to his friend.

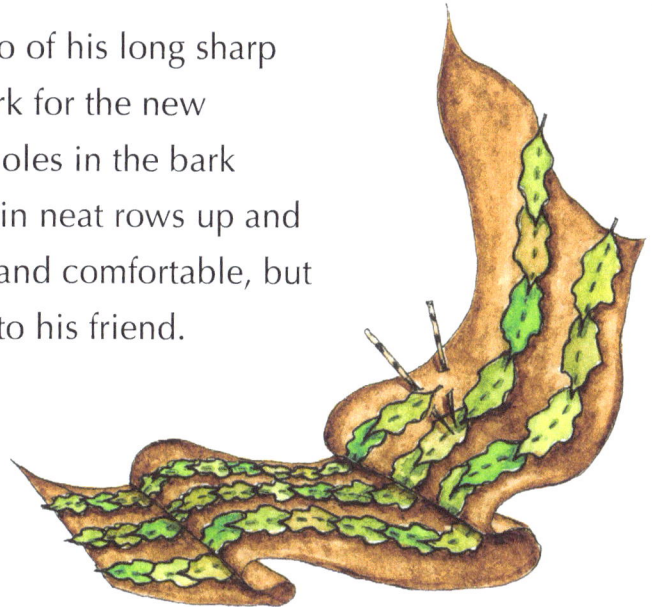

Little Bear and the Mirror

Little Bear was happy to see him and snuggled up under the blanket. All night, he twisted and turned and rolled this way and that way. Alas! Little Bear still shivered and gibbered and jiggled and joggled from the fearful cold.

Squirrel was so unhappy and sighed, "Oh dear! I will have to make a better plan."

Squirrel thought for a moment and said, "I will go and look for some advice from Miss Owl who sleeps in a hole in the tree."

"Miss Owl, Miss Owl, we need your help here please!" Squirrel cried out. Miss Owl does not like to be disturbed during the day when she sleeps, but could hear from the urgency in Squirrel's voice that this matter needed her immediate attention.

"How can I be of help to you my dear?"

Squirrel proceeded to tell Miss Owl the whole story of our shivering, gibbering frightened little bear.

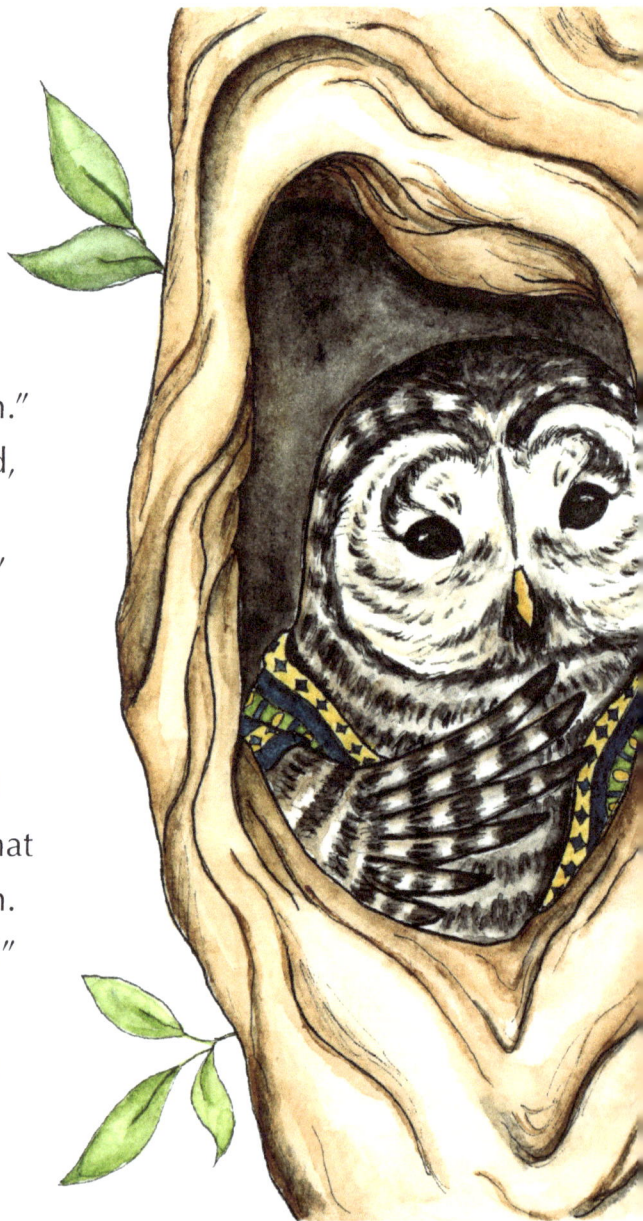

Little Bear and the Mirror

"Oh, this is a big problem," said Miss Owl.
"Let me go inside and read up about Shivering, gibbering fearful cold."

Squirrel was so happy. "You do just that wise Miss Owl. I will wait for your magnificent answers."

Miss Owl opened the scroll of Wisdom Whappers. Down she scrolled, looking for 'gibbering, shivering, jiggling and joggling fearful cold...'

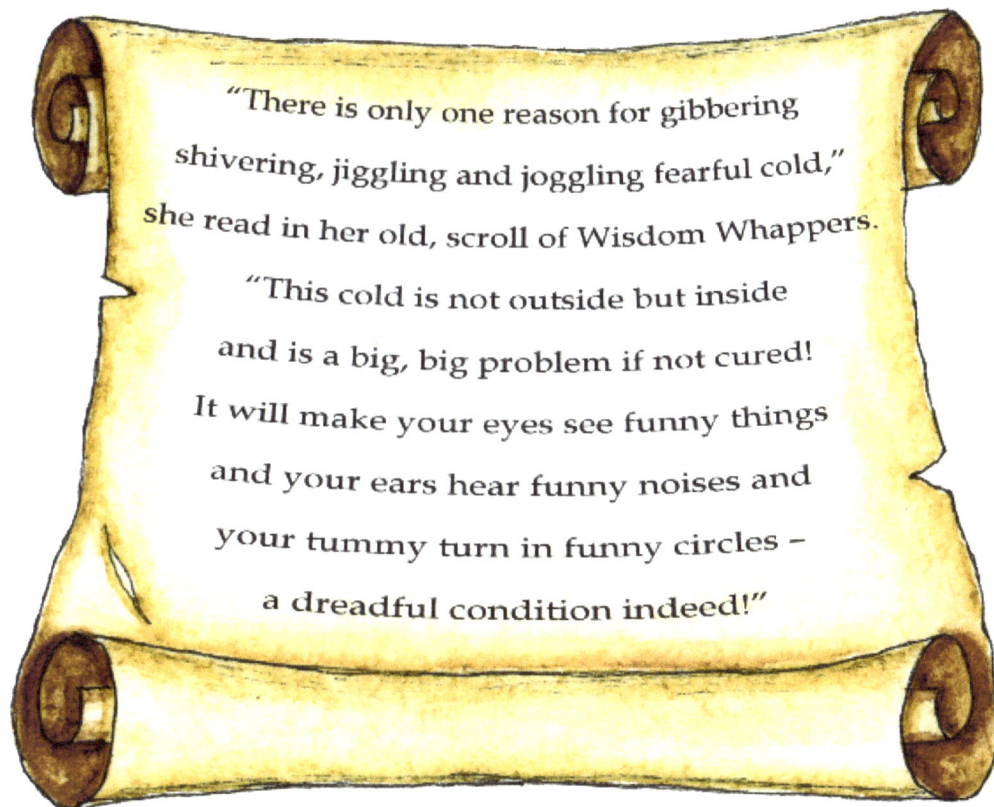

"There is only one reason for gibbering shivering, jiggling and joggling fearful cold," she read in her old, scroll of Wisdom Whappers.

"This cold is not outside but inside and is a big, big problem if not cured! It will make your eyes see funny things and your ears hear funny noises and your tummy turn in funny circles – a dreadful condition indeed!"

Little Bear and the Mirror

Miss Owl wondered to herself, "If the cold is inside and not outside, how can I get what is in, out?" Intrigued by this, she knew there must be an answer, but where to find it!? Down she scrolled and looked and read and mused and then got up to make herself a cup of tea.

"Can I come and help you look for some answers?" Asked Squirrel from below.

"Yes, please, do come and join me," said Miss Owl. And in a wink, Squirrel scooted up to Miss Owl's home. The bookshelves along every wall were filled with reddest red and bluest blue and yellowest yellow books. There were piles and piles of notes stuck against her walls and hanging from the ceiling, was a magnificent wind chime.

Squirrel was intrigued, watching how carefully Miss Owl made her tea. A final little spoonful of honey and a slice of ginger in the cup to give it a very special flavor. Miss Owl says it really helps her to think straight! She sipped her tea delightfully in deep thought and continued to search through her scrolls and books. She hardly looked up – her nose was buried in her work.

Wanting to help, Squirrel grabbed what he thought to be a book, but it was a Mirror! He looked and looked again. "Oh my!!" he said out loud, "It's me! What a handsome specimen I am!" As Squirrel looked and looked, he realized that he looked so much like his daddy and his mommy that he could recognize them right there in the Mirror looking right back at him.

10

Little Bear and the Mirror

Squirrel didn't want our wise friend Miss Owl to know that he could not read, so he just stuck his nose into the Mirror and looked and looked and looked in wonder.

"I've found the answer!" Shouted Owl with great joy. "The cold must get out the same way it got in!"

"Why are you speaking in such riddles Miss Owl? Tell me how we shall do that?" Said Squirrel, perplexed.

"I don't know yet. I need to think. Owls need to think you know. We think with our eyes closed and our heads full of wonderful thoughts. Oh, my goodness that is it!! Scriddly, diddly, dumpchious, exactly that!"

By now, Squirrel could not contain himself and had climbed up the wall and was hanging on the wind chime making it ring a ling, ding a ling until Miss Owl gave him an angry owl look. He immediately came down and sat at the coffee table waiting for Miss Owl's wisdom to unfold.

"The thoughts in our heads become the words in our mouths and then change into the doors that keep in and keep out!!" said Miss Owl, making Squirrel shake his head, still perplexed. "We can make our own thoughts dark and scary when we don't have help," she continued, "They can keep us trapped!"

"You must immediately go back to gibbering, shivering, quivering, shaking, jiggling and joggling fearful cold Little Bear and give him this Mirror."

"Well … actually … I have just been looking at myself and didn't read what is written on the Mirror – because I cannot read!" said Squirrel.

"Well, dear Squirrel, this is not an ordinary Mirror. This is the most wonderful Mirror. It is God's Mirror."

"Oh, my gobbly-wobble-sticks! Does God need a Mirror, Miss Owl?" said Squirrel in surprise.

"No, no, He doesn't need a Mirror, but He wants us to see what He sees when He looks at us, so He gave us a very special Mirror!!

Little Bear and the Mirror

That's it, Squirrel! Now, go take God's Mirror to our fearful gibbering, shivering Little Bear and tell him to look until he sees exactly what God sees. Then he can see what is really true! Then those thoughts that got into his head and made him terribly, fearfully cold…they will unquestionably have to leave!"

"You see, Squirrel, our thoughts are very powerful. The thoughts in our heads are the secret place where all the wonders of the earth are stored, churned, milled, ground and made. But there, we can also hold dark, scary thoughts and lies. Those thoughts turn into words, either good ones or bad ones! We need to know the secret of how to lock in the good thoughts and let them get rid of the bad ones - just like light gets rid of darkness, effortlessly!

Light is stronger than darkness. God's Mirror is His thoughts about us; that's the key!

Little Bear and the Mirror

Squirrel was down in a jiffy – scurrying to his jibbering, jabbering, shivering, little Bear friend. By now, he had thrown the stickily prickly blanket off himself and was sitting, looking like a most miserable, shivering Little Bear.

"I've got good news, Little Bear! Your fearful, shivering days are over!!"

Little Bear's eyes lit up and he leaned forward to see if maybe Squirrel had brought him a nicer, softer blanket. But, oh no, all squirrel had in his hand, was a mirror!

"What's this?" Asked Little Bear.

"It's a magic Mirror," replied Squirrel excitedly. "It lets you see the truth that unlocks the door to let the gibbering, shivering, jabbering, jiggling cold out. Wise owl said the cold could only get out the way it got in!"

So Little Bear, take this Mirror. Look deeply into it."

Squirrel waited with eager curiosity, "Tell me, what do you see?"

Little Bear took the Mirror and gazed deeply. The more he looked, the wider his grin spread along his big bear mouth.

"I see me," said Little Bear.

Little Bear and the Mirror

"Now that's wonderful! Look carefully, what more do you see?" Little bear looked deeper and deeper and saw an amazing secret. "Squirrel! It's like waking up from a dream! I think I see God looking right back at me! Is that possible?"

"Yes!" Shouted Squirrel. "Scriddly, diddly, dumpchious yes! Now you have seen God's Mirror. When you see you and you see Him; He is right there looking back at you, Little Bear!"

"Just think," Squirrel excitedly announced, "God has His home right inside of you and you didn't even know it!
You are His favorite burrow, His favorite honey-pot and His favorite place to be!"

Baby Bear's eyes widened as he listened. He felt a new kind of joy that he had never known before, rumbling around in his tummy. "Tell me more," he said, bumping Squirrel on the arm.

"Well," Squirrel continued, "if God's home is right inside of you, that means He is always with you; even in the scariest times! He loves being with you! You are His friend!

Little Bear and the Mirror

$\mathcal{N}$ow, if scary, cold thoughts come into your head, immediately look in the Mirror and God will help you remember the truth. Just like darkness cannot stay in the light, those old, bad thoughts just cannot stay when you turn on the light of God's thoughts about you! He knows you better than anyone else, and He loves you!"

Little Bear and the Mirror

They heard a "hoot, hoot" in the branches above them. There was Miss Owl, listening with delight to their conversation. She butted right in, "When I make my lovely tea, dear Baby Bear, the little spoon of honey and the slice of ginger, cannot be hidden in the cup. It is what gives the tea such a very special taste! What you have just heard is life's most precious secret. Stir the sweet truth of God's secrets into your thoughts like the churning and swirling of golden honey into your tea. Stir and stir till it's all mixed in! Let it settle in your thoughts Baby Bear and see what happens! This beautiful truth about you, will open the door and chase all those gibbering, shivering, quivering, shaking, jiggling and joggling fearful thoughts right out!"

Little Bear was overjoyed. As he looked into the Mirror and heard these words, he found that he was not cold anymore. He rolled over on his back onto the soft grass, and closed his eyes, completely content. "I am God's home! I am His favorite burrow, His favorite honey pot and His favorite place to be!" He muttered to himself.

"There is that sound again. I can hear it!" he said, as he sat upright. "It's the same sound from the forest that made me scared before, but now it seems like music!" Said Little Bear.

"Oh golly, that is the wind chime in my house" said Miss Owl, delighted! "Little Bear, when the wind blows, the chimes chime and make a tinkling, musical sound. You have nothing to be afraid of anymore," she said laughing with joy!

Little Bear and the Mirror

Little Bear jumped up and did a jiggle, joggle dance of joy and Squirrel joined him, hopping along like a baby kangaroo. They were making such a joyous racket that soon Miss Owl and the other animals of the forest joined them in a merry song and dance.

Now, the forest was filled with this wonderful song!

"Mirror, mirror on the wall, show me the me, that God knows and sees!"

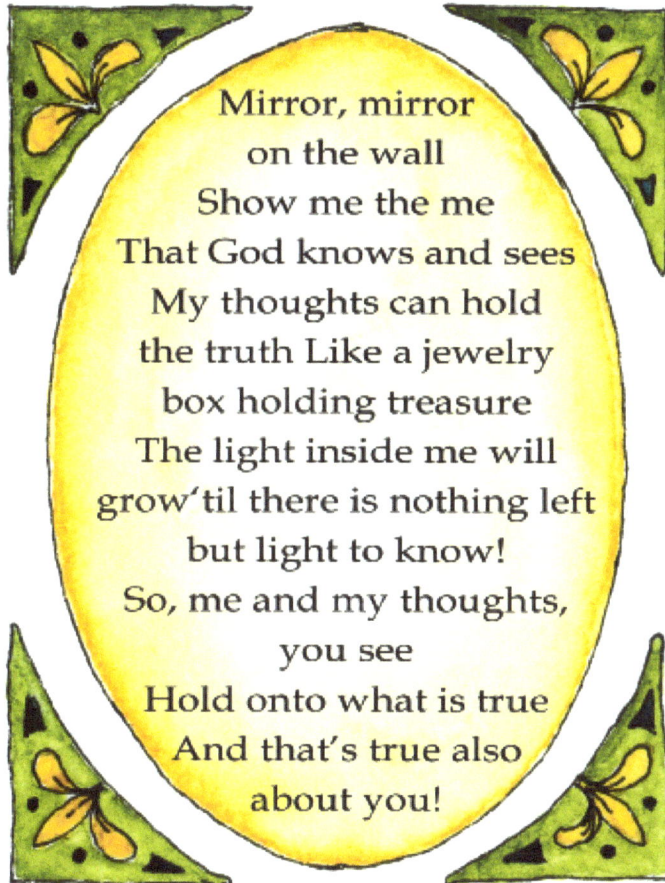

Mirror, mirror
on the wall
Show me the me
That God knows and sees
My thoughts can hold
the truth Like a jewelry
box holding treasure
The light inside me will
grow'til there is nothing left
but light to know!
So, me and my thoughts,
you see
Hold onto what is true
And that's true also
about you!

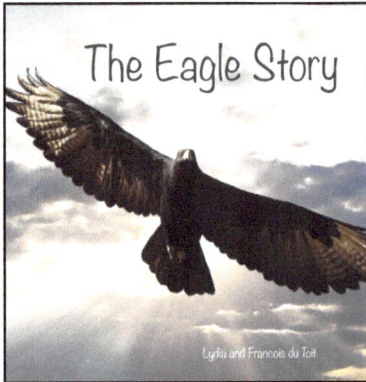

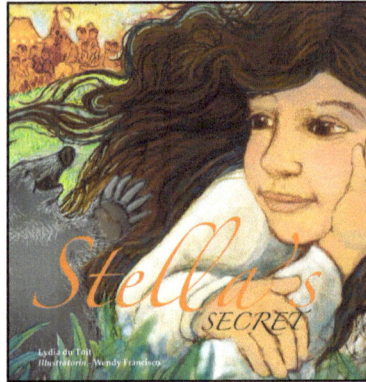

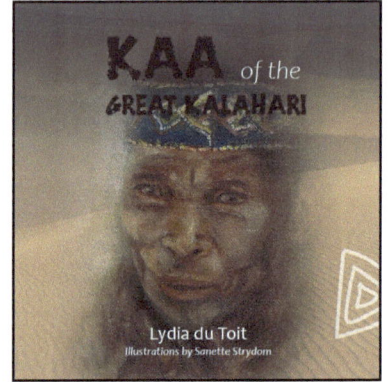

For more amazing children's books by Lydia,
The Eagle Story,
Stella's Secret,
KAA Of The Great Kalahari,
also translated into Afrikaans, German and Spanish

plus free audio links as well as Godfrey Birtill singing
Lydia's Mirror song
please visit our website www.mirrorword.net

www.ingramcontent.com/pod-product-compliance
Lightning Source LLC
Chambersburg PA
CBHW042115040426
42448CB00003B/287